DATE DUE

APR 23 '74			
JAN 9 '75			
SEP 11 '75			
AUG 9 '78			
JUL 4 '79			
DEC 5 '84			
MAR 20 '89			
APR 12 '05			

THE ART OF CHINA

by Shirley Glubok

Designed by Gerard Nook

The Macmillan Company, New York, New York/Collier-Macmillan Publishers, London

Architectural ornament,
Ming (1368–1644),
glazed pottery,
Royal Ontario Museum,
Toronto, photograph
by Alfred Tamarin

The author gratefully acknowledges the kind assistance of:
Lucy Chao Ho, Senior Librarian, The Metropolitan Museum of Art; *Marise Johnson,* Department of Far Eastern Art, The Metropolitan Museum of Art; *Teresa Tsao,* National Palace Museum, Taipei, Taiwan, Republic of China; *Michael Pope;* and especially the helpful cooperation of: *Thomas Lawton,* Assistant Director, Freer Gallery of Art; *John A. Pope,* former Director, Freer Gallery of Art.

Other books by Shirley Glubok:

THE ART OF ANCIENT EGYPT
THE ART OF LANDS IN THE BIBLE
THE ART OF ANCIENT GREECE
THE ART OF THE NORTH AMERICAN INDIAN
THE ART OF THE ESKIMO
THE ART OF ANCIENT ROME
THE ART OF AFRICA
ART AND ARCHAEOLOGY
THE ART OF ANCIENT PERU
THE ART OF THE ETRUSCANS
THE ART OF ANCIENT MEXICO
KNIGHTS IN ARMOR
THE ART OF INDIA

THE ART OF JAPAN
THE ART OF COLONIAL AMERICA
THE ART OF THE SOUTHWEST INDIANS
THE ART OF THE OLD WEST
THE ART OF THE NEW AMERICAN NATION
THE ART OF THE SPANISH IN THE
 UNITED STATES AND PUERTO RICO
THE FALL OF THE AZTECS
THE FALL OF THE INCAS
DISCOVERING TUT-ANKH-AMEN'S TOMB
DISCOVERING THE ROYAL TOMBS AT UR
DIGGING IN ASSYRIA
HOME AND CHILD LIFE IN COLONIAL DAYS

Front cover illustration: *Portrait of a Woman,* anonymous, Ming (1368–1644), color on silk, The Metropolitan Museum of Art, Bequest of George D. Pratt, 1935. Calligraphy by Y. Y. Chang, China Institute.
Back cover illustration: *Children's Play,* hanging scroll (detail), by Su Han-ch'en, Sung (960–1279), ink and color on silk, National Palace Museum, Taipei, Taiwan, Republic of China.

1 2 3 4 5 6 7 8 9 10

Library of Congress Cataloging in Publication Data
Glubok, Shirley.
  The art of China.
  1. Art, Chinese—History—Juvenile literature.
[1. Art, Chinese] I. Title.
N7340.G58   709'.51   72-81059   ISBN 0-02-736170-5

Around 2500—1500 B.C.,
Museum of Far Eastern
Antiquities, Stockholm

China is a huge country in the continent of Asia. It covers a vast area, stretching from the Pacific Ocean to the high mountains of Tibet.

The Chinese civilization, which began more than four thousand years ago, is the oldest living civilization in the world.

Throughout the centuries the Chinese have produced magnificent works of art. Some of their jades, porcelains, paintings, bronzes and silks have never been equalled.

Among the earliest examples of Chinese art are decorated clay pots like the one above. It was made during the Neolithic, or New Stone Age, before the Chinese had learned to use metal.

Around 1100 B.C., Freer Gallery of Art

4

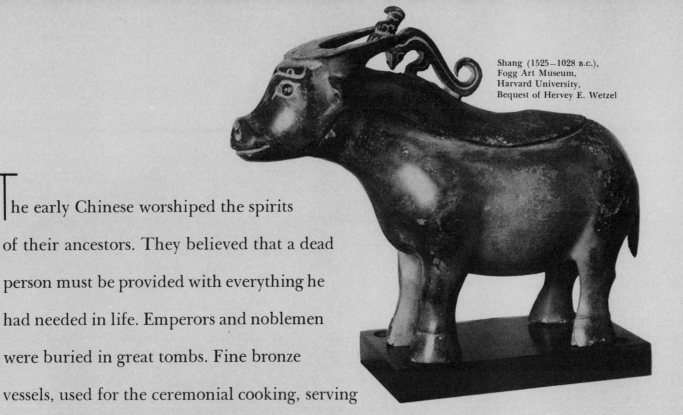

The early Chinese worshiped the spirits of their ancestors. They believed that a dead person must be provided with everything he had needed in life. Emperors and noblemen were buried in great tombs. Fine bronze vessels, used for the ceremonial cooking, serving or storing of food and wine, were placed in the tombs. These offerings to the dead were thought to nourish the souls of the deceased.

Many of the vessels were made in the shapes of animals and birds. The surfaces were decorated with circles, squares and spirals, combined with dragons and animal forms. The designs were thought to be magic and to protect the spirits of the dead.

These bronze animals are ceremonial wine vessels. One is in the shape of an elephant with a smaller elephant standing on the lid. The other represents a water buffalo.

Bronze is a metal composed mostly of copper mixed with some tin and a small amount of lead. When new, the metal is golden brown in color. But most of these vessels have taken on a greenish or blue-greenish color from being buried in the earth for centuries.

The bronze container above, with animal shapes on the lid, is for mixing wine. At far right is a pot for pouring wine. The lid is in the form of a human face with large ears. The bronze owl is also a ceremonial wine vessel.

6

Chinese history is divided into dynastic periods, spans of time during which a country was ruled by a dynasty, a succession of kings or emperors from the same family.

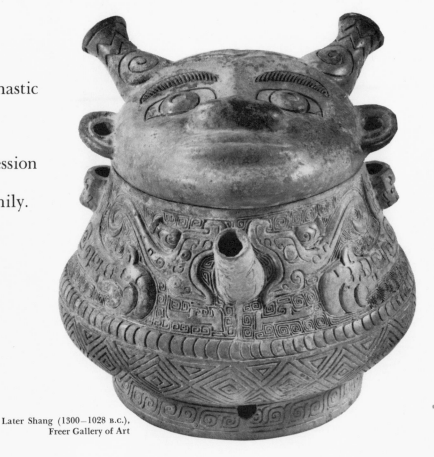

Later Shang (1300–1028 B.C.), Freer Gallery of Art

Around 1027–947 B.C., The Cleveland Museum of Art, John L. Severance Fund

These ceremonial bronzes were made during the two earliest Chinese dynasties: the Shang and the Chou. The Shang dynasty began almost thirty-five hundred years ago and lasted about five hundred years. During this period Chinese writing was invented. The Chou dynasty followed the Shang and lasted more than eight hundred years.

T'ang (618–907),
The Metropolitan Museum of Art,
Rogers Fund, 1910

During the Shang dynasty, when an important man died, some of his servants, guards and household animals would be sacrificed and buried with him. It was believed that they would continue to serve their dead master in his afterlife. In later times pottery, or baked clay, figures were buried instead of real people and animals. Pottery models of houses, carts and other objects were also placed in the tombs to be used in the afterlife. These models give a clear idea of ancient Chinese life and customs.

Camels were used by the Chinese to carry goods across the desert to markets in Central Asia. Below is a cart drawn by a bullock, with a trader and his attendant.

Both of these models were made during the T'ang dynasty, which began almost fourteen hundred years ago and lasted nearly three hundred years. During the T'ang dynasty, the Chinese Empire stretched from Turkey to Korea.

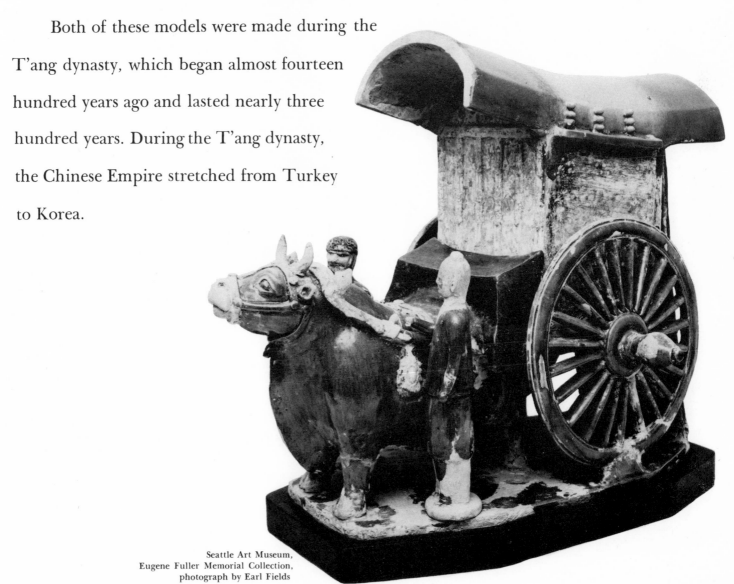

Seattle Art Museum,
Eugene Fuller Memorial Collection,
photograph by Earl Fields

Figures of dancers and musicians were often put into the tombs to entertain the dead. This pottery woman is playing a musical instrument in the shape of a ball.

A great variety of lively horses were made for the tombs. The pottery models were cast in molds. For a human figure the front and back were molded separately, then joined together. Animals were made in several pieces. Some of the objects were covered with slip, or liquid clay, and then painted. Others were colored with glazes, or glassy coatings. The shiny glaze was fused onto the surface of the clay in firing, or baking.

In A.D. 741 an imperial order was issued limiting the number of objects that could be placed in a tomb. The order stated that a high government official might have ninety, but a military leader only ten.

Sui (589–618),
The Metropolitan Museum
of Art, Rogers Fund, 1923

T'ang, Fogg Art Museum, Harvard University, Bequest of Mrs. John Nicholas Brown

Pottery models of buildings tell us a great deal about Chinese architecture. Both private residences and palaces were built with separate structures placed around courtyards. A whole compound might be occupied by several generations of a family. The buildings are surrounded by walls with gates, just as a wall with gates surrounded the city. Bright tiles and ornaments decorate the buildings. Gently curving roofs with upturned eaves extend beyond the walls to protect them from rain.

Sung (960–1279), Museum of Fine Arts, Boston, Hoyt Collection

Watchtowers guarded cities and palaces from attack. People could climb up in the towers and admire the view of the surrounding countryside. The ancient towers were built of wood with tile roofs. They have long since disappeared, but this clay miniature buried in a tomb shows what the towers looked like. It was made during the Han dynasty, which began about two hundred years before the Christian era and lasted about four hundred years. Chinese architecture has changed very little from Han times down to the present day.

Han (206 B.C.—A.D. 220),
British Museum

後周武帝宇文邕在
位十八年五帝興廿五年
毀滅佛法

周武帝楊堅墜在位外

Seventh century, Museum of Fine Arts, Boston, Ross Collection

14

Throughout Chinese history the emperor and his court were important subjects for painters. Yen Li-pen, an artist of the T'ang court, painted the figures of thirteen emperors. At left is Wu-ti, who reigned earlier during the Chin dynasty, with two attendants. The thirteen emperors are painted on a silk handscroll, a long band of silk that is kept rolled up. To be viewed, it is unwound to show one part at a time.

Below is a section of another silk handscroll, illustrating rules of conduct for ladies of the imperial court. An instructress is writing on a handscroll. No background is painted into the picture so our interest is concentrated on the people.

Painting a scroll to teach rules of behavior is in keeping with the views of Confucius, a philosopher who lived about twenty-five hundred years ago. He taught people to be kind, faithful and wise, and to honor their parents.

Attributed to Ku K'ai-chih, Six Dynasties (220–589), British Museum

Chinese people have always been interested in supernatural beings: gnomes, fairies and demons. This scroll illustrates the legend of the Demon Chaser.

According to the story, an emperor had been troubled by a small demon that crept into the palace, stole a flute and danced about, playing it. A bearded man appeared and captured the demon. The man, whose name was Chung K'uei, was rewarded by the grateful emperor. He was given the office and title of "Great Spiritual Demon Chaser of

The Demon Queller, by Kung K'ai,
thirteenth century, Freer Gallery of Art

the Whole Empire," and spent his time finding and

destroying evil spirits.

In this scene Chung K'uei and his sister are being

carried in litters. With them are their attendants and

enslaved demons. The Demon Chaser looks backward to

be sure everyone is following him properly.

This handscroll is painted on paper, which was

invented in China early in the second century A.D., nearly

two thousand years ago.

Landscapes are a favorite subject for Chinese painters. It is believed that an energy or spirit in nature breathes life into all things, and the painter must capture this spirit in his painting to give it life. Landscape scenes rarely represent actual places. They are usually created out of the artist's imagination.

In *Mountain Pass After Snow* the artist T'ang Yin has created a towering composition. The whole space is filled with steep mountains, deep gorges and tumbling waterfalls. A path winds through the snow-covered valley, inviting the viewer to take an imaginary walk through the painting. Tiny figures of people are included to show that man is but a

Early sixteenth century, ink and color on silk, National Palace Museum, Taipei, Taiwan, Republic of China

small part of the natural world. Taoism, one of the major beliefs in China, teaches that man is of little importance compared to mountains, rivers and waterfalls.

This landscape painting is a hanging scroll, which can be unrolled and hung on a wall. A hanging scroll is a vertical composition; a handscroll is horizontal.

Below is a scene from a handscroll of life on a river. Fishermen are busy in their little boats, while a family picnics on the bank. The artist Tai Chin painted this active scene of people and nature with the fewest possible strokes of the brush.

Handscroll (detail), fifteenth century, ink and color on paper, Freer Gallery of Art

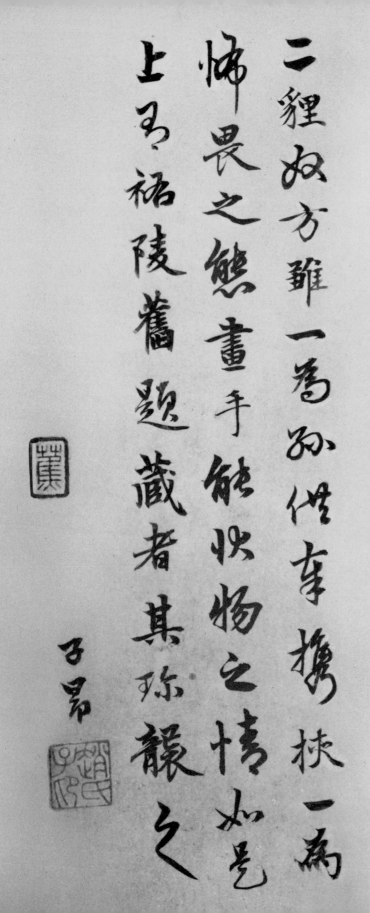

All Chinese artists are trained in calligraphy, or brush writing. Calligraphy is considered a fine art, like painting; the same methods and materials—brushes, inks and paper—are used for both.

Water is put on an ink stone. Then an ink stick, or solid slab of ink, is rubbed on the stone. Ink grinds off the stick and mixes with the water to make liquid ink. The artist uses a flexible hair brush, which may be held upright or slanted to vary the stroke. The pressure on the brush controls the thickness of the lines. The movement of the hand is swift and continuous.

Chinese script is written from top to bottom, in columns that go from right to left. Many different dialects are spoken in different areas of China, but everyone reads the same script.

Inscription on a painting,
Yüan (1279–1368), National Palace Museum,
Taipei, Taiwan, Republic of China

The painting of bamboo plants is closely related to calligraphy. The movement and pressure of the brush in forming the leaves and stalks is like the brush stroking used to form the characters in calligraphy. The artist must have perfect control. He must know when to press the brush and when to lift it. The bamboo artist must give the feeling of a living plant, with leaves swaying and branches gently bending.

This bamboo painting, as well as the calligraphy, is by Chao Meng-fu. He outlined a rock with rapid strokes of his brush. An old stump, with bare branches, stands out against the graceful stalks of the living plant. The springing movement of the young branches, with their pointed leaves, was painted with rapid brush strokes.

The bamboo plant is both flexible and strong. To the Chinese, it symbolizes the qualities of a true gentleman.

Hanging scroll, ink on silk,
National Palace Museum, Taipei,
Taiwan, Republic of China

Color on silk, Museum of Fine Arts, Boston, Japanese and Chinese Special Fund

The Emperor Hui-tsung of the Sung dynasty was an artist as well as a collector of fine

works of art. This painting by the emperor shows ladies busily working with silk.

It is a detail of a handscroll and is a copy of an earlier work that is now lost. It was

part of the training of a Chinese artist to copy the works of earlier masters.

For hundreds of years the Chinese were the only people who knew how to raise the

worms that produce silk, the finest natural textile known to man. Silk thread is strong

and elastic. Silk cloth is soft, warm and easy to dye.

Silkworms are raised by farmers under highly controlled conditions. They are fed

specially grown mulberry leaves. After a few weeks the worms spin cocoons. When the

moths emerge, the cocoons are unwound to get the threads from which cloth is woven.

Silk robes decorated with embroidered patterns of silk threads were worn by the emperors and their officials as a symbol of their high rank. Below is a dragon robe, which was worn in the emperor's court.

According to legend, precious silkworms were smuggled out of China during the sixth century in the headdress of a Chinese princess.

K'ang-hsi period (1662–1722),
Royal Ontario Museum, Toronto

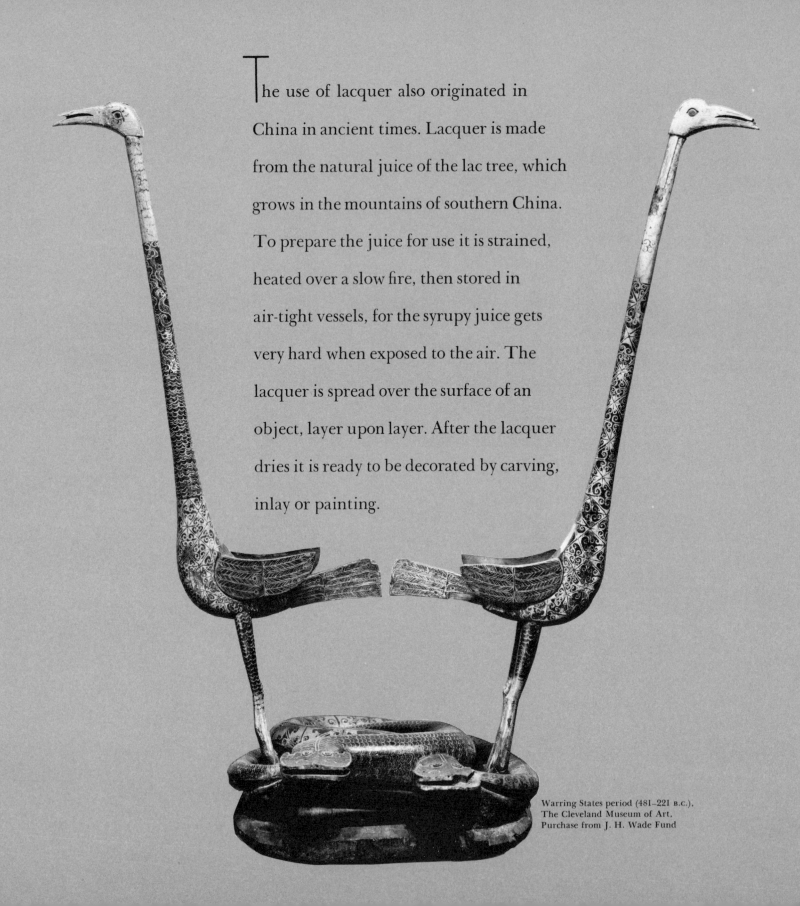

The use of lacquer also originated in China in ancient times. Lacquer is made from the natural juice of the lac tree, which grows in the mountains of southern China. To prepare the juice for use it is strained, heated over a slow fire, then stored in air-tight vessels, for the syrupy juice gets very hard when exposed to the air. The lacquer is spread over the surface of an object, layer upon layer. After the lacquer dries it is ready to be decorated by carving, inlay or painting.

Warring States period (481–221 B.C.),
The Cleveland Museum of Art,
Purchase from J. H. Wade Fund

Lacquer is extremely poisonous. People who work with it must develop an immunity to it. Lacquer is resistant to water, heat and acids. The cranes at left are of wood covered with painted lacquer.

To the Chinese, jade is the most precious of all materials. Since ancient times it has been used in religious ceremonies for both the living and the dead. Jade has always been loved and honored, and thought to possess magical powers.

There are two varieties of jade: nephrite, which is white in its purest form, and jadeite, which is bright green.

Jade is smooth to handle and cool to touch, but soon becomes warm in the hand. One of the hardest of stones, it is very difficult to work. Since it is too hard to carve or cut, jade has to be shaped by the slow process of grinding and rubbing. When it is worked very thin, light will shine through it.

The stag and the round object with a hole in the center are both ancient jades that were buried in tombs.

Warring States period, Nelson Gallery-Atkins Museum, Kansas City, Missouri (Nelson Fund)

Around 500 B.C., The Metropolitan Museum of Art, Rogers Fund, 1924

25

Around tenth century, The Brooklyn Museum,
Ella C. Woodward and Frank L. Babbott Funds

The Chinese discovered the secret of manufacturing porcelain more than a thousand years ago. Porcelain is made by combining kaolin, a fine white clay, with feldspar, a crystalline rock. The word *kaolin* comes from the name of a hill where deposits of this special clay were found. Nearby a whole city grew up based on the manufacture of porcelain.

Porcelain is smooth, hard and—although light in weight —quite sturdy. Porcelain vases and plates are made on a potter's wheel. They are glazed, then fired at a very high steady temperature—about three thousand degrees Fahrenheit—for a long period of time.

Porcelain became a valuable item for trade with Europeans. Great quantities of it were taken to Europe, where it was called "china." It took more than seven hundred years for Europeans to discover the secret of making porcelain.

Above is a porcelain pitcher with a spout in the shape of a phoenix, a mythical bird. At right is a large storage jar with a fierce dragon encircling it. The color for the designs was made from cobalt, a mineral that produces a brilliant blue.

宣德年製

Fifteenth century,
The Metropolitan Museum of Art,
Gift of Robert E. Tod, 1937

27

1210, ink and color on silk,
National Palace Museum,
Taipei, Taiwan, Republic of China

This duck vessel and the imperial dog cage are examples of cloisonné enamelware. The objects are copper with enamel decoration. Designs were outlined with raised copper wire, creating cloisons, or little cells. The cells were filled with colored enamel made from finely ground powders. Then the objects were baked in a kiln, or very hot oven.

Ch'ien-lung period (1736–1795), National Palace Museum, Taipei, Taiwan, Republic of China

The charming drawing at left is the *Knickknack Peddler,* by Li Sung. The peddler, carrying five hundred articles, is showing his wares to a mother and her children. The little ones seem delighted with the peddler's goods. The lively figures were drawn with fine lines.

This picture is an album leaf, a single picture framed by a border of silk.

Ch'ien-lung period, Philadelphia Museum of Art, Gift of the Friends of the Museum

Beggars and Street Characters, album leaves mounted as handscroll, 1516,
ink and color on paper, The Cleveland Museum of Art, John L. Severance Fund

Chou-ch'en, a Ming dynasty artist, painted unfortunate

people dressed in ragged, tattered clothes. Such characters

are an unusual subject for Chinese art.

A crippled beggar screws up his face in pain, while

strolling entertainers perform tricks with their trained animals.

There is no background in the picture. The viewer is

expected to know that the scene takes place on a village street.

In Ma Yüan's album leaf painting at right, an old man

follows two donkeys loaded with charcoal and firewood.

Nature forms a quiet background. Large areas of the painting are bare,

but the branches on the right direct attention toward the figures.

The painter Ma Yüan came from a family of artists. His great-grandfather,

grandfather, father, uncle, a son and nephews were all painters.

Through Snowy Mountains at Dawn, Sung, ink and color on silk,
National Palace Museum, Taipei, Taiwan, Republic of China

Hanging scroll, Sung, ink and color on silk,
National Palace Museum, Taipei, Taiwan, Republic of China

Chinese painters often portray animals and birds. The rabbit surrounded by a variety of wild flowers and the mother hen with her chicks were painted by anonymous, or unknown, artists.

The squirrel jumping onto a peach branch is by Ch'ien Hsüan. The little animal with its bushy tail is not much bigger than the peach. Every knot on the branches and every vein of the leaves is drawn realistically.

Handscroll, late thirteenth century, ink and
color on paper, National Palace Museum,
Taipei, Taiwan, Republic of China

Two seals of the artist have been stamped on the painting. Five hundred years later an emperor who then owned the handscroll put his own seal on it. He also wrote a poem about the squirrel and the peach across the painting. It was common practice for a painter to write a poem or remarks on his own painting; then friends and later admirers added their own seals, signatures or thoughts.

Hanging scroll, Sung, ink and color on paper,
National Palace Museum, Taipei,
Taiwan, Republic of China

Horses have always been highly prized in China. Owning horses was a symbol of wealth, and they were used for the cavalry, for hunting and polo, and for pageants, parades and circuses. Fine steeds were sent to the emperors as gifts from foreign rulers, and expeditions went out to Central Asia to collect horses for the imperial stable. One emperor had more than four thousand horses in his stable. The animals were so important that court artists were often called upon to paint their portraits.

This detail, or part, of a hanging scroll shows eight men mounted on handsome, spirited horses. The rider in the center leans forward, raising his crop, while most of the other riders look toward him. The faces of the sportsmen are drawn to show their individual characters.

Eight Gentlemen on a Spring Outing, attributed to Chao Yen, Five Dynasties (907–960), National Palace Museum, Taipei, Taiwan, Republic of China

Three Horses and Four Grooms, handscroll (detail), ink and color on silk,
The Cleveland Museum of Art, Purchase, Leonard C. Hanna, Jr., Bequest

In the thirteenth century the Chinese were conquered by the Mongols,

from Central Asia, who were known for their horsemanship. Two of the great

Mongol emperors were Genghis Khan and Kublai Khan. Genghis Khan was the

conqueror of China. Kublai Khan, his grandson, became famous in Europe

through the writings of Marco Polo, a Venetian explorer who visited China

during his reign. The period when the Mongols ruled China was the Yüan dynasty.

The horse with two grooms was painted by Jen Jen-fa during that period. The figures are clearly outlined.

Fine dogs were also brought into China from Central Asia. The two Saluki hounds were painted by Hsüan-te, an emperor of the Ming dynasty, the period after the Mongols had been driven out of China. The artist-emperor painted the lean figures of the dogs, their silken hair and long looping tails without outlining their bodies. The flowers help to balance the composition.

1427, color on paper, Fogg Art Museum,
Harvard University, Gift of Charles A. Coolidge

Ming (1368–1644), Royal Ontario Museum, Toronto

Buddhism, a religion which began in India, was introduced into China around the first century A.D. The life and teachings of the Buddha became important subjects for Chinese art.

Born Prince Siddhartha, in India, the Buddha grew up in a palace, protected from the outside world. One day he rode out from the palace and was shocked by the misery he saw—old age, sickness and death. He made up his mind to go out into the world and to find out why human beings suffer and how they could be free from pain. For many years he wandered and meditated, seeking the answer. One night, seated under a fig tree, he went into a deep trance. When dawn broke he reached Enlightenment; he saw the innermost secrets of birth and death. It was then that he was given the name Buddha, which means "The Enlightened One," or "He Who Knows All Things." With his new knowledge and understanding he spent the rest of his life walking the earth preaching.

Buddhist temples have been built all over China. Statues of the Buddha and his followers fill the temples. The large bronze Buddha at left is seated on a lotus blossom, which is a symbol of Buddhism. The beautiful lotus flower rises from the mud of slimy ponds, as Buddha's teachings arise from the misery of the world.

Chinese Buddhists also built pagodas, tomb monuments in the shape of towers, with projecting roofs at each story. At right is the Marble Pagoda, just outside Peking, the present capital of China.

Eighteenth century,
photograph Library of Congress

Eighth century, The Cleveland
Museum of Art, Gift of Mr. and Mrs.
Severance A. Millikin

Bodhisattvas are beings of complete enlightenment who have dedicated themselves to relieving the misery of the world. The most popular Bodhisattva is the kind and gentle Kuan-yin, goddess of mercy.

The wooden Kuan-yin at right sits in a relaxed and graceful pose. She is dressed in costume and jewelry that a royal person might have worn. In the center of her crown is a tiny figure of Buddha.

This eleven-headed Kuan-yin is made of sandstone. The large rounded face is peaceful and kindly. Some of the other heads are angry.

The Kuan-yin's ear lobes are very long, a sign of royal birth. Royal persons wore large earrings that stretched the lobes of their ears.

Late twelfth century, The Art Museum,
Princeton University, photograph by Alfred Tamarin

41

Early Buddhists in China cut cave temples into the living rock. At Lung-men in Honan in northern China the gray limestone cliffs are carved with hundreds of Buddhist figures, both inside and outside the caves. Some of the carvings are only a few inches tall; others are colossal.

This is a view of the main cave temple at Lung-men. The three large figures, from left to right, represent a Bodhisattva, a guardian of the Buddhist faith and a heavenly king.

672–675,
photograph by Paolo Koch,
Rapho-Guillumette

43

On a lake surrounded by mountains outside Peking is the Imperial Summer Palace. Its magnificent buildings and gardens were the emperor's country residence. This bronze dragon stands outside the Throne Hall of the Summer Palace. The dragon is a symbol of power and good luck and it is said to bring rain to crops. It was also a symbol of the emperor. The imperial dragon had five claws, while other dragons had only three or four.

At left is the Hall of Annual Prayers in Peking, the central building of the great Temple of Heaven. Once a year, at the beginning of spring, the emperors would come here and spend the night fasting, then praying for good crops.

The wooden building has three curved roofs of bright blue tile. This triple dome is a symbol of heaven.

Nineteenth century, photograph Library of Congress

Built 1420—rebuilt 1754,
photograph by Paolo Koch,
Rapho-Guillumette

The festival of *Ch'ing Ming,* which means "clear and bright," takes place every spring in China. On this day people plant trees to honor their dead relatives.

A handscroll almost thirty-three feet long follows this festival along the Yellow River. The scenes begin in the country in the early morning and continue to the market place and into the city with its crowds of people. Included in the scroll are shops, parade grounds, bridges and temples. An archery contest and a birthday party are also shown.

In this detail the walls and gates of houses can be seen. Boats move along the river. On the far side of the river, mules pull loaded carts while horsemen, pedestrians, peddlers and a toy vendor pass by.

This scroll gives a clear picture of how people lived in China. For hundreds of years, until the early twentieth century, this way of life changed very little.

Ming, anonymous, color on silk,
The Metropolitan Museum of Art,
Fletcher Fund, 1947

The Demon Queller (detail),
Freer Gallery of Art

In 1912 the rule of the Chinese emperors ended. The last imperial dynasty, the

Ch'ing, was overthrown and the Republic of China was established. After years of civil

war and foreign invasion, the Chinese Communists gained control of most of the

country. In 1949 they founded the People's Republic of China on the mainland, and the

government of the Republic of China moved to the island of Taiwan.

The Chinese have deep respect for their ancestors and pride in their history.

This feeling for their past and a love for the beauty of their land have always been

reflected in Chinese art. Other civilizations have flourished and then disappeared, but

Chinese culture and many of its traditional art forms are still alive after more than

four thousand years.